Recipes for Hemp Seeds

Hemp

The #1 Superfood on the Planet

Ryder Management Inc.

Copyright © 2015 Ryder Management Inc,

All rights reserved.

ISBN – 10: 1508402191
ISBN-13: 978-1508402190

Epigraph

"Hemp is of first necessity to the wealth & protection of the people".
Thomas Jefferson

"Make the most of the Indian hemp seed, and sow it everywhere!"
George Washington in a note to his gardener, 1794, Mount Vernon

Table of Contents

Hemp i

The #1 Superfood on the Planet i

Epigraph iii

Table of Contents v

Introduction-The Nutrition in Hemp Seeds 8

Recipes 11

    Blueberry Banana Hemp Smoothie 11

    Hemp Seed Milk 12

Garlic and Hemp Seed Oil Salad Dressing 14

Hemp Ginger Dressing 16

Hemp Seed Ranch Dip/Dressing 17

Creamy Hemp Dressing/Dip 18

Smooth Hemp Carrot Dressing 20

Cajun Hemp Sauce 21

    Baked Sweet Potato Fries 22

    Cajun Spice 23

Hemp Pesto 24

Hemp and Basil Pesto 25

Benefits of Basil 26

Hemp Butter 27

Garlic Toast with Hemp Butter or Pesto 28

- Benefits of Garlic 29
- Hemp Humus 30
- Hemp Seed Tomato and Parsley Salad 31
- Vegetarian Hemp Seed Chili 32
- Veggie Hemp Chili 34
- Hemp Stuffed Sweet Potatoes 36
- Hemp Seed Chicken Fingers 36
- Hemp Desserts 39
- Creamy Chocolate Hemp Avocado Pudding 39
- So Delicious Chocolate Hemp Pudding 40
- Hemp Seed Banana Bread 41
- Hemp Soup 42
  - Hemp Carrot Soup 42
  - Hemp Spinach Soup 44
  - Hemp Borsht Soup 45
- Other Ideas to Incorporate Hemp into Your Daily Diet 47
- Hemp Fun Facts 48
- Online Organic Hemp Sources 51

Introduction to The Nutrition in Hemp Seeds

Did you know that hemp seed (from the industrial hemp plant) is THE true superfood found in nature? This natural food source was taken away from the people due to its connection to "marijuana". The fact is there is no THC content in hemp or hemp seeds – the food source of industrial hemp.

Hemp seeds have the ultimate nutritional ratio between omega-3 fatty acid and omega-6 fatty acid being roughly three to one (3:1). In addition, hemp seeds are rich in Gamma-Linolenic Acid (GLA), an important Omega-6 fatty acid. GLA is capable of healing inflammation, inhibit cancer cell growth and improve skin, hair and nail health. Essential fatty acids are very important to healthy cells in our brains, heart, skin and virtually every system in the human body making hemp the ultimate super food.

In addition to the above, hemp seeds contain very high levels of Vitamin A, C, E and beta carotene. Hemp seeds also contain an abundance of iron, magnesium and potassium and are also rich in protein, carbohydrates, and other minerals along with fiber. Hemp food also contains calcium, vitamins B1, B2 B3 and B6 and D. It is also interesting to note that there has never been one reported allergy to hemp seeds.

Just four tablespoons (Tbsp.) or 56 grams of shelled hemp seed provides 72% of the recommended daily allowance (RDA) for Vitamin E. According to Dietitians of Canada, Vitamin E "helps to maintain a healthy immune system and other body processes. It acts as an antioxidant and protects cells from damage." Four tablespoons in the course of a day is not that much. If we increase the quantity to 100 grams or 6 tbsp. and 2 tsp. We will have exceeded the recommended daily requirement of Vitamin E.

According to the European Industrial Hemp Association, 100 grams of shelled hemp seeds contain 90% of the RDA of Vitamin B1 (thiamine) and 30% or the RDA for Vitamin B3 (Niacin).

Dieticians of Canada report that Vitamin B1 (Thiamin) "helps with energy production in our bodies" and Niacin (Vitamin B3) helps our bodies to utilize protein, fat and carbohydrate in making energy. Niacin also helps enzymes to properly work in our bodies.

Hemp seeds also contain all 20 amino acids, including the ten essential amino acids our bodies are unable to produce on their own. The amino acid, Edestin, is only available in hemp and has been found to be an integral source in our DNA. Hemp is made up of two important globular proteins 65% edestin (a Greek word meaning edible), and 33% albumin which have structures very similar to proteins made by the blood, which makes hemp readily digestible. This alone, makes hemp the closest plant based source of protein. No other food source provides such a complete protein in such an easily digestible form, not even soy. Soy protein content is fairly difficult to digest.

Hemp foods contain all eight essential amino acids, Leucine, Lysine, Threoine, Phen+tyro, Valine, Meeth+cyst, Isoleucin, Tryptophan, with higher amounts of each than any other main sources of protein including egg whites, tofu, human milk, and whole cow's milk. Besides these 8 essential amino acids, hemp foods also provides the necessary types and amounts of amino acids the body needs to make serum albumin and serum globulins, two other amino acids essential to life. All of this makes hemp a complete source of protein.

Shelled or hulled hemp seeds have a very mild nutty flavor and are the perfect garnish for soups, salads, stir-fries, puddings, oatmeal and yogurt, to name, but just a few.

Hemp seeds can also be ground into hemp milk, the recipe of which is in this book. In addition, hemp seed oil (cold pressed to ensure its nutrients are retained) can be used in oil-pulling for improved dental health, or in salad dressings, pesto, pancake mix, granola, and so much more.

Hemp is a plant with a long history of use that dates bake to the beginning of time. George Washington and Thomas Jefferson were two US Presidents and hemp farmers. In the 1600's, the US government mandated settlers to grow hemp in order to help them to thrive and survive.

Unfortunately, as a result of the criminalization of industrial hemp, in favor of cheaper petroleum products and by-products during the early 20th century, a lot of the true history of hemp including its plethora of uses, as well as hemp breeding has since been lost or destroyed.

Hemp seed was criminalized for nothing other than greed from a small group of influential whites that used the racism of the day as a way to scare people away from this plant altogether. Hemp and its THC rich cousin threatened the evolving early twentieth century industries including paper, plastic, pharmaceutical, naval supply stores, to name just but a few. However, this history is beyond the scope of this book.

This book provides recipes that utilize this sacred super food in our everyday meals in order that we can, once again, use this super food, a gift from above, to regain, retain or obtain our health, the way we were always meant to.

Recipes

Blueberry Banana Hemp Smoothie

Ingredients:

1 banana

½ cup frozen blueberries

5 Tbsp. hemp seeds, shelled

1 cup almond or hemp seed milk

¼ tsp cinnamon powder

¼ tsp ginger powder

½ tsp Ashwagandha, optional

½ tsp Maca, optional

Directions:

Add all ingredients to your NutriBullet tall cup or other high speed blender and blend until smooth (approximately 60 seconds.) This recipe is so smooth and very rich in nutrients including energy boosting properties; you will want this every morning.

If you don't have a high speed blender, you may want to use hemp seed flower in your other blender to obtain the full nutritional benefits from this recipe.

Serves 1

Hemp Seed Milk

Ingredients:

1 cup hemp seeds, shelled

5-6 cups purified or filtered water

Natural sweetener such as up to 2 Tbsp. **or** raw honey, raw coconut sugar **or** pure maple syrup

Or 4 pitted dates, soaked

Optional Ingredients:

1 tsp natural organic vanilla extract, optional

1 Tbsp. non-GMO lecithin, optional

1 Tbsp. virgin coconut oil, optional

Pinch of Himalayan salt, optional

Instructions:

Place all ingredients into your NutriBullet Tall cup or your Vitamix or similar high powered blender.

Please note that the optional lecithin and coconut oil will add a richer and creamier product.

The dates, raw honey, raw coconut sugar or maple syrup will add a sweeter taste and the vanilla extract will also aid in resembling the store bought, without any additives.

Consume unstrained for the most nutritional benefits, however, you can strain in a nut bag for a smoother consistency. Nut milk bags are available at most health food stores such as online at Truly Organic Foods.

If you do choose to strain the pulp, save it for use in cookies, pancakes or other baking.

This mild hemp seed pulp can be added to ½ cup of fresh blueberries, one banana and a dash of cinnamon and blended for a delicious smoothie for two.

Garlic and Hemp Seed Oil Salad Dressing

The following recipe can be adjusted to suit your taste by substituting red wine vinegar or freshly squeezed lemon or lime juice for the apple cider vinegar. Apple cider vinegar was chosen specifically for its own health and healing benefits. In addition, it is your choice how much or whether to include turmeric powder to this recipe. Adding a smidgeon (1/4 tsp) will increase this recipe's powerful immune boosting ability.

To make the perfect dressing, remember that the ratio of hemp seed oil to apple cider vinegar (or lemon or lime juice) is three to one (3:1). With this ratio in mind, you can adjust this recipe to the number of guests you're serving. The basic recipe follows and will serve four.

Ingredients:

3 Tbsp. Hemp seed oil

1 Tbsp. Apple cider vinegar (ACV)

1 clove garlic, peeled and crushed

¼ tsp turmeric powder

Crushed black pepper corn

Himalayan pink salt (HPS)

Directions:

Whisk together the Hemp oil and ACV (oil and vinegar) with the crushed garlic and turmeric powder.

Add crushed black pepper and HPS (at least 1/8 tsp of each) to start.

Taste and adjust salt and pepper to taste.

Serve over a fresh spring mix, spinach salad or greens of your choice

Hemp Ginger Dressing

Ingredients:

2 Tbsp. hemp oil

2 Tbsp. Sesame Oil

1 Tbsp. rice vinegar

1 inch or peeled and chopped fresh ginger root

2 tsp tamari or soy sauce

Directions:

Whisk all ingredients together in a small bowl or alternatively, blend in your NutriBullet small cup

Chill before serving.

This recipe makes approximately ¼ to ½ cup dressing.

Hemp Seed Ranch Dip/Dressing

This is one delicious dip for cut veggies or as a dressing for salads.

Ingredients:

½ cup Greek yogurt

½ tsp dried basil

½ tsp dried thyme or dill

1 tsp parsley

1 clove garlic, peeled and minced

6 Tbsp. Hemp seed oil

3 Tbsp. hemp seed, shelled

¼ tsp Maple syrup

½ tsp Himalayan pink salt

½ tsp Ground pepper

Directions:

Add all ingredients to a high speed blender or food processor until smooth and creamy

Makes 1 cup

Serve chilled with fresh cut veggies or mixed with your favorite salad greens.

Creamy Hemp Dressing/Dip

Ingredients:

½ cup hemp seeds, shelled

½ cup filtered water

2 Tbsp. nutritional yeast (available from health food stores)

2 Tbsp. fresh squeezed lemon or lime juice

1 garlic clove, peeled and minced

¼ to ½ tsp Himalayan pink salt

¼ tsp turmeric powder, optional

1/8 tsp fresh ground pepper

Directions:

Add all ingredients into your high speed blender or NutriBullet tall cup and blend until creamy and smooth, approximately 60 seconds.

Taste and adjust seasonings to suite your taste

Chill before serving as a dip as it will thicken.

Alternatively, serve immediately over your favorite salad.

This dressing will keep in the refrigerator for at least a week if covered and sealed in an air tight container.

Once chilled, this dip is very tasty served surrounded by fresh cut veggies, pita or pumpernickel bread pieces for dipping.

Put in a preheated oven for a full 13-15 minutes then remove from the oven and turn all the fries over.

Put back in the oven for an additional 7-10 minutes.

Baking the fries for the full 15 minutes on one side and ten on the other will give you crisp fries that are slightly dark.

Serves two and is delicious served with Cajun Hemp Sauce as a dip.

Smooth Hemp Carrot Dressing

Ingredients:

¼ cup hemps seeds

2 Tbsp. hemp oil

2 large carrots, peeled and chopped

½ cup filtered water

¼ cup apple cider vinegar

1 cup Arugula or spinach leaves

2 tsp paprika

½ tsp turmeric

½ tsp Himalayan pink salt

1/8 tsp fresh ground pepper

1 Jalapeno pepper, seeded and chopped

Directions:

Combine all ingredients in your NutriBullet small cup or other high speed blender or food processor.

Blend until creamy and smooth, approximately one minute.

This dressing will keep in the fridge for up to three days if sealed.

Serve tossed with your favorite salad.

Cajun Hemp Sauce

Ingredients:

¼ cup cold pressed hemp seed oil

½ cup plain Greek yogurt

4 Tbsp. tamari sauce

2 Tbsp. Cajun spice

1 Tbsp. fresh ground pepper

1 pinch cayenne powder

Himalayan salt to taste

Directions:

Combine all ingredients into a mixing bowl and mix well

This sauce is a great dressing for vegetables, salads, pasta or meat.

This recipe is also a delicious dip when served with sweet potato fries.

Baked Sweet Potato Fries

Ingredients:

1 large sweet potato

Coconut oil

Himalayan pink salt

Fresh ground pepper

Olive Oil, optional

Directions:

Preheat oven to 450 degrees F.

Scrub the sweet potato and then cut both ends off.

It is important that the potato is completely dry

Peeling the sweet potato is optional

Cut the potato in half and cut each half into large slices about ¾ inches thick.

Cut the above into ½ inch pieces. Your fries should now be ½ inch to ¾ inches thick.

Spread evenly on a greased baking sheet using coconut oil.

Sprinkle generously with Himalayan salt and ground pepper

Drizzle a good quality virgin olive oil over the top and shake your baking sheet to mix thoroughly.

Once everything is mixed, evenly space the fries out on the baking sheet and ensure that none are touching.

Cajun Spice

Cajun spice can easily be made at home. The following recipe makes ¼ cup of a spicy Cajun spice that can be stored in an airtight container:

Ingredients:

2 tsp Himalayan pink salt

2 tsp garlic powder

2 ½ tsp paprika

1 tsp ground black pepper

1 tsp onion powder

1 tsp cayenne pepper

1 ¼ tsp dried oregano

1 ¼ tsp dried thyme

½ tsp red pepper flakes, optional

¼ tsp turmeric, optional

Directions:

Stir all ingredients together until well blended.

Store in an airtight container

Hemp Pesto

Ingredients:

1 cup of fresh, washed basil leaves, chopped

½ cup Hemp seeds, shelled or hulled

¼ cup cold pressed hemp seed oil

½ cup Parmesan cheese, grated or chopped

Himalayan pink salt and ground pepper to taste

Directions:

Combine basil leaves, hemp seeds, and Parmesan cheese in a NutriBullet tall cup or other high speed blender and blend, while slowly adding the hemp seed oil.

Blend until desired consistency is reached.

Taste and adjust fresh ground pepper and Himalayan pink salt, to your liking.

Suggestions:

Spread on pizza dough before adding other ingredients

Toss with cooked pasta and sautéed vegetables

Spread on baguette slices, top with cheese and grill

Add hemp seed oil to thin for a salad dressing

Hemp and Basil Pesto

Ingredients:

3 cups fresh basil leaves

1/2 cup hemp seeds (shelled)

3 Tbsp. freshly squeezed lemon juice

1-3 garlic cloves, minced

1/2 tablespoon black pepper

1/2 teaspoon Himalayan pink salt

1/2 cup cold pressed hemp seed oil

Instructions:

Rinse the basil leaves and add to your NutriBullet or other speed blender.

Add the hemp seeds, lemon juice, garlic, salt & pepper and ½ the hemp seed oil.

Blend until smooth, adding additional oil until desired consistency is reached.

Makes 2 cups and will store in the refrigerator for up to two weeks in a sealed container.

Suggestions:

Use lime juice or apple cider vinegar as an alternative to the lemon juice.

This recipe is delicious on pizza, pasta, rice noodles or as a sandwich spread.

It is also delicious served with crackers and pita chips.

This recipe can be kept in the fridge for up to five days.

Benefits of Basil

One half cup of basil is an excellent source of Vitamin K and Manganese. This same quantity also provides a very good source of copper, Vitamin A and Vitamin C. In addition, it is a good source of calcium, iron, folate, magnesium and omega-3 fatty acids.

Incorporating this annual plant into your daily or weekly diet has many health benefits that are beyond the scope of this short book.

Hemp Butter

Ingredients:

1 cup Hemps seeds, shelled or hulled

2 Tbsp. cold pressed hemp seed oil

Directions:

Place both ingredients in your NutriBullet short cup or other high speed blender

Blend until creamy smooth or desired consistency is obtained (30 – 60 minutes).

This recipe may require you to scrape the sides of your blender a few times until you do reach the desired consistency.

Any unused amount can be stored in a sealed container in the refrigerator.

Garlic Toast with Hemp Butter or Pesto

Ingredients:

Hemp butter or Hemp Pesto

Gluten free bread, sliced thick

1 or more cloves of garlic, peeled and minced

Cheese of your choice (such as white cheddar, parmesan, mozzarella, goat, etc.)

Directions:

Using either your prepared hemp butter or hemp pesto, stir in one or more cloves of minced garlic for added health benefits.

Spread about 1 tsp of the hemp mixture onto your favorite crusty bread or roll.

Top each piece with grated cheese of your choice, if desired.

Place garlic bread onto a cookie sheet or rack.

Place under the broiler for a few minutes until the top is toasted or grilled according to taste.

Serve immediately

Benefits of Garlic

Garlic has powerful antibacterial, antiviral, antifungal and antiprotozoal properties making it an antimicrobial natural antibiotic. The allicin in garlic is what makes it a true antibiotic found in nature. Garlic is known for its ability to inhibit a large number of bacteria at bay while assisting our good bacteria in this defense.

Garlic is also a natural defense against a number of known parasites. Although a number of pharmaceutical drugs have been synthesized for this purpose, none are as effective as garlic.

Garlic has a number of other benefits in addition to that previously described, it is interesting to note that there are no known side effects when using garlic in large quantities, other than an aroma some people may experience while taking certain pharmaceutical drugs.

The alliinase enzymes found in garlic can further enhance its health properties if let to sit a few minutes after chopping or mincing. In other words, if you let your chopped, minced or crushed garlic a few minutes to rest prior to changing its temperature through cooking or its pH by adding apple cider vinegar or lemon juice, research has shown that its medicinal and other health benefits are increased.

Garlic consumption has been shown to be effective against so many illnesses and diseases. In fact, this discussion is beyond the scope of this book. Suffice it to say that, garlic should be on of your staple foods, for optimum health.

Research is now reporting too, that garlic also has the ability to regulate the fat content in our bodies.

Hemp Humus

Ingredients:

3 cups chick peas

½ cup hemp seeds

¼ cup hemp seed oil

2 cloves garlic, peeled and chopped

¼ cup fresh squeezed lemon or lime juice

2 Tbsp. fresh chopped parsley

2 Tbsp. cumin powder

2 tsp. turmeric powder

1 tsp Himalayan pink salt

1 tsp fresh ground black pepper

½ - 1 tsp cayenne pepper

Directions:

Combine all ingredients in a high speed blender or food processor.

Blend until mixture reaches your desired consistency adding more hemp oil as necessary

Serve chilled, surrounded by fresh cut veggies, pita strips, pumpernickel bread and/or crackers.

Top with additional hemp seeds and fresh chopped chives, if desired

This dip can be kept, sealed, in the refrigerator, for up to four days.

Hemp Seed Tomato and Parsley Salad

Ingredients:

For the salad:

1 bunch of Italian Flat Parsley, chopped

½ medium sweet onion such as Vidalia, chopped

1 medium tomato, diced

½ medium cucumber, diced

6 heaping Tbsp. hemp seeds, shelled

Dressing:

Juice of one lemon

1 clove garlic, peeled and minced

Cold pressed hemp seed oil

Himalayan pink salt, to taste

Directions:

Chop the parsley and add to your salad bowl along with diced tomatoes, chopped onion, and cucumber and hemp seeds.

Whisk together the dressing ingredients and pour over salad.

Toss salad to taste and adjust seasoning.

Vegetarian Hemp Seed Chili

Ingredients:

1 Tbsp. coconut oil

1 medium onion, chopped

1 garlic clove, peeled and minced

3 cups of diced tomatoes

1 green, red or yellow pepper, seeded and chopped

1 cup hemp seeds, shelled

½ cup distilled or filtered water

2 Tbsp. chili powder

1 tsp turmeric powder (or more)

1 tsp cumin powder

1/8 tsp cayenne pepper

½ tsp fresh ground black pepper

1 can kidney beans, drained and rinsed

1 can black beans, drained and rinsed

1 jalapeno pepper, seeded and chopped, optional

Directions:

Heat oil in a large saucepan over medium heat
Add onion and garlic and sauté until soft, approximately two minutes
Stir in the remainder of the ingredients except the hemp seeds and bring to an almost boil.
Reduce heat to low and continue to cook for an additional 20-30 minutes, adding water if chili becomes too thick
Just before serving, add in the hemp seeds and heat through.
Taste and adjust seasoning as necessary, before serving.

Veggie Hemp Chili

Ingredients:

1 Tbsp. coconut oil

1 medium onion, chopped

2 medium carrots, peeled and chopped

1 small green pepper, seeded and chopped

1 garlic clove, peeled and minced

3 ½ cups tomato sauce

1 cup of vegetable stock or filtered water

1 15 oz. can of chick peas, drained and rinsed

1 15 oz. can of kidney beans, drained and rinsed

2 Tbsp. chili powder

1 Tbsp. turmeric powder, or to taste

1 tsp Himalayan pink salt

1 tsp fresh ground pepper

½ cup hemp seeds

Directions:

In a large pot over medium heat, stir and sauté onion in coconut oil for 1 minute

Stir in carrots, peppers and minced garlic and continue to stir and sauté for an additional three minutes

Stir in remaining ingredients, except the hemp seeds, and then cover and simmer for one hour

Taste and adjust seasoning according to taste.

Just before serving, stir in ½ cup of hemp seeds and stir an additional minute or two.

Top each serving with a teaspoon of mashed guacamole mixed with hemp seeds plus an additional sprinkle of hemp seeds or hemp seed flakes.

Hemp Stuffed Sweet Potatoes

Ingredients:

1 or 2 large Sweet Potatoes

1 -2 Tbsp. Hemp oil, cold pressed

1-2 Tbsp. Hemp seeds, shelled

½ -1 tsp Himalayan pink salt

1 -2 tsp of fresh or dried dill

Fresh ground pepper to taste

Directions:

Preheat oven to 350 degrees F.

Wash and scrub sweet potatoes and poke with a fork.

Bake at 350 F for 30 minutes or until soft when touched.

Remove from oven and let cool slightly.

Cut the sweet potato length wise.

Scoop out 80% of the sweet potato center and add to a mixing bowl.

Add to the bowl the hemp oil, hemp seeds and salt and pepper and mix well.

Taste and adjust seasoning.

Divide the mixture and return to the sweet potato skins.

Top each with another sprinkle of hemp seeds and serve.

Each half serves one.

Hemp Seed Chicken Fingers

These chicken fingers are easy to make and are kid friendly AND very nutritious.

Ingredients:

1 package of organic boneless chicken breasts

½ cup gluten free bread crumbs

½ cup coconut flour

¼ cup hemp seed, shelled

½ cup parmesan cheese, grated

1 ½ tsp Himalayan pink salt

1 tsp dried thyme

1 Tbsp. fresh basil, chopped or 1 tsp dried

¼ tsp turmeric powder

1/8 tsp fresh ground pepper

½ cup hemp oil

Directions:

Preheat oven to 350 degrees

Trim and cut chicken breasts into strips

Line baking sheet with parchment paper or grease with coconut oil

Pour all dry ingredients into a large bowl and mix well

Soak cut chicken strips in hemp oil

After strips are coated with oil, transfer to large bowl and coat all sides

Place coated strips onto baking sheet in rows and bake at 350 degrees for 20-25 minutes or until juice runs clear.

Remove from oven and let cool slightly before serving with honey.

This recipe also goes great with Hemp Seed Ranch Dip as an additional dipping sauce.

Hemp Desserts

Creamy Chocolate Hemp Avocado Pudding

Ingredients:

2 ripe avocados, halved, skinned and pitted

¼ cup of carob powder

¼ cup hemp seed, shelled

1 Tbsp. maple syrup or coconut sugar

¼ tsp cinnamon powder

¼ tsp ginger powder

1/8 cup almond, coconut or hemp milk or filtered water

Directions:

Combine all ingredients into your NutriBullet tall cup or Vitamix or other high powered blender and blend until smooth, approximately 30-60 seconds.

Add additional milk or filtered water for desired consistency if necessary

Place in the freezer for approximately 10-15 minutes to chill through.

Serve in dessert bowls topped with a sprig of mint or quartered grape

Serves 2-3

So Delicious Chocolate Hemp Pudding

Ingredients:

1 cup hemp seeds, shelled

2 Tbsp. Cacao or carob powder

¼ cup coconut sugar **or**

10-12 medjool dates, pitted for a natural sweetener

½ cup filtered water or hemp, almond or coconut milk

¼ tsp ginger powder

¼ tsp cinnamon

Pinch of nutmeg

Directions:

Put all ingredients into your NutriBullet small cup or other high speed blender

Blend until rich and creamy, additional water, if necessary

Put in the freezer for 10-15 minutes until chilled through

Serves 2-3

Hemp Seed Banana Bread

Ingredients:

2 eggs

1/3 cup apple sauce

2/3 cup of coconut sugar

2 cups coconut flour

2 ¾ tsp baking powder

½ tsp Himalayan pink salt

1 cup mashed bananas

¼ cup hemp seeds, shelled

¼ cup carob or cacao nibs, optional

Directions:

Preheat oven to 300 degrees F.

Mix first three ingredients with mixer or in a blender until smooth.

Add dry ingredients alternating with mashed bananas and continue to blend until smooth.

Pour into a greased loaf pan (9 x 5 or similar).

Bake for 45-60 minutes until a clean toothpick comes out clean.

Remove from oven and let cool before turning out on a rack.

Hemp Soup

Hemp Carrot Soup

Ingredients

¼ cup hemp seed oil

4 Tbsp. hemp seeds

3 carrots, peeled and chopped

½ medium onion, chopped

1 celery stalk, chopped

1 inch of fresh ginger root, peeled and chopped

1 garlic clove, peeled and chopped

¼ tsp Himalayan pink salt

1/8 tsp fresh ground pepper

¼ tsp turmeric powder

3 cups of filtered water, heated separately in a tea kettle or pot

Fresh avocado, peeled, pitted and cubed, for topping, optional

Fresh cut chives, for serving, optional

Directions:

Combine all ingredients, except avocado, in a high powered blender.

Blend until creamy and smooth, approximately 60 seconds or more

Taste and adjust seasoning and temperature according to taste.

If a hotter soup is desired, reheat just before boiling.

Serve topped with fresh chopped avocado, additional hemp seeds and chives, if desired.

Hemp Spinach Soup

Ingredients:

4 cups loosely packed organic spinach leaves

1 ½ Tbsp. freshly squeezed lemon or lime juice

1 Tbsp. extra virgin hemp seed oil

2 Tbsp. chopped green onions or chives

1 ½ cup vegetable stock or filtered water, heated

¼ cup hemp seeds, shelled

¼ to ½ tsp Himalayan pink salt

1/8 tsp turmeric powder, optional

Fresh ground pepper

Directions:

Put all ingredients into a high speed blender such as a NutriBullet or Vitamix, and blend for 30 to 60 seconds until smooth or desired consistency is reached.

Taste and adjust seasoning and re-heat if necessary.

Serve topped with an additional tsp of hemp seeds and chopped green onion or chives

Hemp Borsht Soup

Ingredients:

2 Tbsp. coconut oil or hemp seed oil

½ cup Hemp Seeds, hulled (seeded)

3 cups Beets, peeled and chopped, shredded or slivered (approximately 3-medium beets)

2 large carrots, peeled and chopped, shredded or slivered

3 cups filtered water

1 large avocado, peeled, pitted and chopped

1 small onion, chopped

2 cloves garlic, peeled and slivered

1/3 cup fresh squeezed lemon or lime juice

1 Tbsp. tamari, optional

Directions:

Combine all ingredients, except the beets, in a high powered blender such as a NutriBullet or Vitamix.

Blend until smooth and creamy, approximately 60 seconds.

Borsht can be served hot or cold.

If you prefer this soup hot, gently reheat on a low temperature while stirring in the chopped, shredded or slivered beets.

Heat until the beets are heated through, approximately five minutes.

Serve with fresh chopped chives, dill and additional hemp seed, if desired.

Other Ideas to Incorporate Hemp into Your Daily Diet

Hemp seeds are a perfect protein, as they contain all the necessary amino acids. They are a perfect source for energy, for satisfying hunger, improving digestive health, for weight loss and for improving tissue health. Healing Source (healingsource.com) reports that consuming 88 grams of hemp seeds daily (ideally with other long fiber foods and avoiding starch-prominent, machine-predigested foods); will improve health dramatically in a very short time.

Following are suggestions for increasing the amount of hemp in your daily diet:

Blend 2-5 Tbsp. into your morning shake for an extra boost of energy;

Take your hemp seeds with you when dining out in order to add to your meal for an extra boost of nutrition;

When making wraps, pitas or any sandwich, be sure not to forget to add hemp seeds for additional nutrition and an energy boost;

Add to your ground beef when making burgers, lasagna, shepherd's pie, or any pasta sauce and dish;

Mix in with your potato salad recipes, tossed green salads and other vegetables;

Add as a topping to soup;

Spread over your morning toast;

Eat straight from a spoon;

Add as a topping to your morning breakfast cereal.

Hemp Fun Facts

The word "hemp" comes out of Western Europe as a description of a number of varieties of the cannabis plant, particularly the varieties of industrial hemp, that were bred over time for specific uses including building material, fuel, fiber, rope, paper, canvas, seed, food, oil and so much more. A number of items stocked at the navy supply stores of prior centuries were made of hemp.

The cultivation and use of hemp dates back over 12,000 years and while it was native to Asia, it was grown in, and had an enormous influence upon many of the ancient and more modern cultures and on the history of Europe and America.

It was legal to pay taxes with hemp in America from 1631 until the early 1800's. The reason to make hemp legal tender was a way to encourage farmers to grow more.

Refusing to grow hemp in America during the 17th and 18th centuries was actually against the law. You could be jailed in Virginia for refusing to grow hemp from 1763-1769.

Hemp was the first crop to grow in many American states. In 1850, Kentucky was producing 40,000 tons. Hemp was used in 80% of all textiles, fabrics, clothes, linen, drapes, bed sheets, etc. Hemp was a very useful and a crop that produced farmers with a steady income.

In 1916, the U.S. Government predicted that by the 1940s all paper products would come from hemp and that no more trees would need to be cut down. Government studies report that only one acre of hemp was equivalent to 4.1 acres of trees. Plans were in the works to implement such programs to utilize hemp. However, major paper companies had other plans. (During the years 1916-1937, William Randolph Hearst created a yellow journalism campaign to associate hemp with marijuana, thus banning both completely) *from hemp.com*

ABOUT THE AUTHOR

Ryder Management Inc. *(Rydermgt or RMI)* is a Canadian Controlled Private Corporation (CCPC) based in London, ON Canada. As an "umbrella" organization, RMI brings together a group of authors whom are professionals in their respective fields and are writing with the primary goal of providing books that educate, comfort and offer assurance that natural health remedies do exist and are an effective and safe way to regain, obtain and maintain health.

Ryder Management Inc. "putting you in gear" can be found on line at rydermanagement.ca

Online Organic Hemp Sources

Healing Source: http://www.healing-source.com/

Healing source is an excellent source for organic hemp seed s, flakes, and powder, oil, salad dressing, and hemp protein bars.

Truly Organic Foods: http://www.trulyorganicfoods.com/

Truly Organic Foods is an online source for healing foods including hemp powder, hemp seeds and hemp oil.

Printed in Great Britain
by Amazon.co.uk, Ltd.,
Marston Gate.